I0076775

Praise For *Dive Into Strengths*

"This little gem of a book has quickly made its way to my must-read list! Rhonda's passion for helping others discover and utilize their talents more effectively is unmistakable in this hands-on guide that will take you on your own strengths journey."
Steven Ligon, Director of Career Advancement for
BHHS Anderson Properties of Oklahoma

"This book is a great way to learn how to apply the StrengthsFinder test to the real world. After reading this book, I then highly recommend attending the workshops provided by the Yellow Sub Group -- whether you live in Oklahoma City or not! This is the best way to ensure you will be the best YOU that you can be!"
Sean McDuffie, Entrepreneur/Musician

"Rhonda brings her own incredible insight into the Clifton Strength Finder, Upon completion of the exercise that Rhonda put together I became more aware of how I utilize my strengths in my daily activities. This is a fantastic tool that I will continue to use.
Rodney Lewis, Business Broker

"If you have lived life wondering why you consistently struggle in certain areas of life, you need to read this book. It is perfect for the beginner who is ready to remove the blinders and finally become aware of who they truly are."
Veronica Ray, Jigsaw & Associates.
"You are blind as a bat to how awesome you are!"

"What next? Too often in my experience, well intended authors and/ or speakers take me to a new level, a new 'ah-ha!' and then leave me there wondering what to do next. For me, that is the great gift of Rhonda's book and what makes it different. She gives me the insight and lift of a StrengthsFinder evaluation but doesn't leave me there. 'Dive into Strengths' is just that, a journey to cultivate an awareness and practice of living into my strengths in all areas of my life. Actually living my strengths not fighting my weaknesses! What a liberating gift to give indeed."
Brian Perry, Hindsight Life, Atlanta, GA

Dive Into Strengths
An Exploration of the Very Best YOU

by Rhonda Knight Boyle

Dive Into Strengths

Published by:
Yellow Sub Publications
4917 N Portland Avenue
Oklahoma City, OK 73112
rhonda@yellowsubgroup.com

http://YellowSubGroup.com

Copyright 2016 © Rhonda Knight Boyle
Cover Designed by: Jamie Batac

All rights reserved. No part of this publication may be reproduced or transmitted
in any form or by any means, including informational storage and retreival
systems, without permission in writing from the copyright holder, except for brief
quotations in a review.

ISBN 13: 978-0692719275

Dedication

This book is dedicated to my favorites in the community: small business owners, entrepreneurs, independent sales representatives and consultants from all industries. YOU are the visionaries and the drivers who love freedom above all things. You're willing to strive for the best, work tirelessly, and sacrifice in order to build something great and long-lasting.

This book is also dedicated to those who believed in me from the beginning. You know who you are. You kept encouraging me, kept challenging me, and kept forwarding my thinking into dynamic possibilities. Thank you for being part of my journey!

To my family: Chris, Alli and Laura. You all know me in my strengths -- and my lesser talents. I love you and am grateful that you've put up with me all these years!

And to three other special people in my life --

Lee Collins with Ruthless Marketing, for planting the first seeds…. And kicking my hiney to execute my Big Ideas.

Diane Hochman, who I found when I clicked on that link and fell down that rabbit hole….

And to you, dear Reader, as you begin your Strengths-based journey. THIS is the work of your life!

Rhonda

Disclaimer:

The non-Gallup information you are receiving has not been ap-
proved and is not sanctioned or endorsed by Gallup in any way.
Opinions, views and interpretations of StrengthsFinder results
are solely the beliefs of Rhonda Knight Boyle and Yellow Sub-
Group.

Introduction

First Things: My Story or Discovery, or something like that...

For many years, I've had a high interest in psycho-metrics, the branch of study in measuring human psychology. It all started with Florence Littauer's, Personality Plus, which pulled on the historical first descriptors developed by Hippocrates, hundreds of years BC/BCE.

Hippocrates developed the first ever personality test. Believe it or not, he did it through autopsies! True story. He studied the "bile in the blood" of the people he knew who had died. Over time, he came up with four "types" of people.

He described four temperaments by the following names and descriptions:

Phlegmatic

Those who are Phlegmatic in temperament are often private and inwardly focused. They may have high principles and integrity. They are often patient, kind, calm and adaptable. They roll with the punches of life and everybody loves them.

Choleric

Those who are temperamentally Choleric are no-non-sense go-getters. They are usually task-oriented and focused on efficiency. They are often ambitious and love to be in charge of things. They are usually the immediate leaders in any given situation.

Melancholic

Those who are Melancholic in temperament are often super introverts. They may be serious, cautious, suspicious, or detail-oriented. They are also focused, conscientious, and like to work independently.

Sanguine

Those with the Sanguine temperament are usually playful and fun. They are often talkative and highly sociable. They are optimistic, imaginative and they make new friends easily. They can energize others and forward others' thinking.

I came to a deep understanding of these four temperaments and learning them helped me have a greater understanding of other people. I discovered how each temperament reacted to circumstances and used this information to coach others on how to work within their area of comfort.

Most modern-day personality tests focus on the same (or similar) four quadrants, although most have dropped Hippocrates' four difficult-to-pronounce temperaments (they're a mouthful, aren't they?). Today, you can find a plethora of personality tests -- some label you with colors, some give you letters, and in others you can be identified by an animal avatar that shares some of your characteristics.

The greatest purpose of these assessments is behavior modification. The theory goes like this: if I know enough about each personality type and their descriptors then I will be able to modify MY behavior to meet THEIR needs.

The trouble is we don't often do that.

In the field of Psychometrics, there are a number of types of assessments and I'm certain I've taken them all at one point or another. However, the greatest value for me has been in seeing the characteristics in others in an effort to know them better. To help meet their needs.

The only problem I faced was I could never apply it any further in my own life. I learned, for example, that as a Sanguine, I was NOT well suited for statistics, reports or long-term planning. I also clearly gravitated towards people and events and activities that were busy, productive and FUN! I also knew I didn't have to be in charge of things, either. I was quite happy as long as there was a "party" feel -- lots of high energy and quick action!

But that still didn't tell me HOW I did things and never kept me from getting stuck behind the 8-ball of a deadline, frantically trying to pull together the information that someone needed. It didn't stop me from wasting my time and energy waiting for someone else to make things happen. I was always "chomping at the bit" to get moving.

In spite of all my studies and knowledge, there were too many questions that needed answers. So, I continued to take new assessments as they came out in an effort to find solutions.

Strengths-based Movement

In 2008, my faith community implemented a new stewardship program called Living Your Strengths, based on the book by Albert Winseman, Donald Clifton and Curt Liesveld. It was eye-opening!

We each took the new Clifton StrengthsFinder 2.0 assessment released in 2007 by the Gallup Corporation. Then, through small group participation, we were able to discuss our newly discovered Top Five talents and their descriptions.

What was different in this psychometric assessment was that it was NOT just a personality test. No, not at all. It didn't deal with Hippocrates' Four Temperaments either. Instead, the Clifton StrengthsFinder 2.0 assessment identified raw talent and potential strength.

Not only that, they had a decidedly different view about human potential. Those involved in the Strengths-based movement had the belief people are at their best when they maximize their strengths rather than trying to fix their weaknesses.

Wow! The thought of that was freeing!

I was worn out trying to fix my weaknesses. From the beginning of my childhood memories, I can remember teachers and counselors and other well-meaning people telling me and my parents (often in parent-teacher conferences) that I was not living up to my full potential.

Apparently, I talked too much, wiggled too much, didn't turn in work in a timely manner, forgot my homework, didn't do well on long-term research projects, and on and on. By the time I entered high school, I chose to take the easiest classes so that I no longer had to deal with that negative feedback. I became an expert at choosing the courses that I would excel in -- and I did. I achieved nearly all A's, with an occasional B, and I skated my way into the top 15% of my class at graduation.

I threw off any formal continuing education. College? Why would I waste any more time on an academic environment that did not fit my needs, was dry and boring and that forced me to learn things in which I had absolutely no interest?

So when I took the StrengthsFinder 2.0 assessment, I thought, "Finally! Someone gets ME!" followed quickly by, "How'd they know that?"

I was intrigued and wanted to learn more. That began

a journey of nearly eight years at the time of this publication.

The StrengthsFinder Details

The Clifton StrengthsFinder 2.0 assessment was the lifelong work of Donald O. Clifton, an American psychologist and professor of educational psychology at the University of Nebraska. Clifton is known as "The Father of Strengths Psychology" and also the "Grandfather of Positive Psychology" according to the American Psychological Association.

Clifton's company, Selection Research, Inc., purchased the Gallup Corporation in 1988. Since then, the assessment has also become known as the "Gallup StrengthsFinder Assessment."

This body of work was nearly forty years in the making when the assessment was finally released to the general public in a book by the same name, StrengthsFinder 2.0, by Tom Rath. It is still on best seller lists today -- nine years after being published.

The theory behind the book and the assessment is that there are at least 34 identifiable "talent clusters" known as Signature Themes. While Gallup concedes that there are likely more, these 34 talents are observable and measurable personal character attributes.

The StrengthsFinder 2.0 assessment consists of 177 questions asked every 20 seconds, with the opportunity for the participant to determine how strongly they do (or do not) agree with pairing statements. After 25-45 minutes, you are rewarded with a list of the top five talents you live in. This is where you experience the greatest potential for developing your raw talents into strengths.

Your Top Five Signature Themes -- also known simply as the "Top 5" -- are the areas where you already show promise. You're currently operating in these talents whether you recognize them or not.

If you haven't already taken the StrengthsFinder 2.0 assessment, you can do so by going to:

www.GallupStrengthsCenter.com.

Get started by purchasing your Top 5 Signature Themes report. Unlocking all 34 of your talents will prove beneficial later.

Once you learn your Top 5 talents and how they show up in your own life, you get the opportunity to embrace them. Then you can explore new ways to intentionally lean into them -- on purpose -- again and again and again!

Through this process you will create a life by your own design.

A life where you live to your fullest potential!

A life where you get to do what you do best!

A life where you get the most positive energy!

A life where you get the most satisfaction!

A life of being the very best version of yourself!

I'm excited just thinking about the journey you're about to embark upon! And I'm delighted to be with you during these next steps.

Please do not hesitate to contact me with any questions. I'm here to serve you!

Rhonda Knight Boyle
Yellow Sub Consulting Group
www.YellowSubGroup.com
www.Facebook.com/YellowSubGroup
770-317-6408

Chapter One:

Identify Your Potential Strengths

After taking the Gallup StrengthsFinder 2.0 assessment, you will have been given five new words to identify the talents within you that have the most intensity.

Again, StrengthsFinder 2.0 is NOT a personality test. It is a talent assessment.

Your Top 5 talents have been revealed through the answers you provided. YOU told the test your patterns of thought, feelings and behaviors. These talents are like your signature, your method of operation, the lens through which you view the world. If you were a computer, it would be your operating system.

This is the way you view the world! Through these Top 5 talents, you've lived your life since you were very young -- who knows, maybe even as young as 5 or 6. These talents were inborn in you and over time -- through your environment, your education, your training and experience -- these have been strengthened to the point they provide your greatest potential for excellence.

This is your "Strengths Zone." This is the space you can shine. This is the place where you can dominate, where you can most likely do things better than 10,000 other people! This is the area where you are at your best, your most productive, your most vibrant, your most... EVERYTHING.

In fact, you're so good at them you don't even know that you're doing them. It's like looking through your own eyeballs -- you don't even think about them when you're in action. You are always looking out of your own eyeballs.

So go take a look at your results again. What are the five new words that you have been given to claim for your own?

List your Top 5 talents here:

_____

_____

_____

_____

_____

Chapter Two:
Discover Your Strengths

Now that you have your Top 5 talents (which are just words at the moment), it's time to discover what they all mean.

Each of your Top 5 talents comes with a description, explaining the "cluster" of talents that may or may not be strong in you. Not every talent description will match you exactly.

Some words may pop out at you and you'll say, "Yes! That is SO ME!" Others, not so much. It may be "close but no cigar," or "If only it had said, 'this' instead of 'that', it would be perfect."

And that's exactly right because YOU are the one who gets to determine exactly WHO you are and how YOU do things.

So let's get to work on discovering who you are, shall we?

Go back to www.GallupStrengthsCenter.com and look at your results again. Print your Strengths Insight and Action-Planning Guide provided free by Gallup. With each of your Top 5 talents, read the description and then write the words or phrases from the guide that resonate with you the most here:

Talent: _____

Words and phrases that resonate _____

_____

_____

Talent: _____

Words and phrases that resonate _____

_____

_____

Talent: _____

Words and phrases that resonate _____

_____

_____

Talent: _____

Words and phrases that resonate _____

_____

_____

Talent: _____

Words and phrases that resonate _____

_____

_____

Chapter Three:
Explore Your Strengths

Now is the time to be watchful and observant. Now is the time for you to catch yourself in action.

You see, you're already really, really good at using your talents. In fact, you're so good at using them, and they've become such a part of your life, that you don't even notice when you're using them. You are blind as a bat as to how awesome you are!

You can't see it because they are a part of you; a living, breathing part of you. You're not looking for it at all.

Instead, you are looking at what you think you're do-ing wrong and everything that needs fixing in your life. You focus on the negative, on the things you can't do well.

You're critical of the fact you often leap before you look. Or maybe you are accused of being lost in a fog because you think too much. Maybe someone has suggested that you talk too much or you're too friend-ly. You're too pushy, too quiet, too loud, too sensitive, too nosey, too negative, too positive, too something.

You're constantly comparing yourself to others and either find yourself ahead (which gives you some con-solation) or behind (which creates lots of stress).

If you're like me -- and I know that you are human, and therefore you are -- you've been told your whole life that, if you'll just work on your weaknesses you'll be successful.

Your parents told you this.

Your teachers told you this.

Your bosses told you this.

And your whole life you've followed this "weakness fixing" mentality. You've worked harder and harder on these miserable little parts of your life and you've never, ever seen much progress.

These weaknesses follow you around wherever you go. After all, there's no escaping yourself.

Are you worn out yet? How much longer do you have to keep working on your deficits?

With the information you've now been given through the Gallup StrengthsFinder 2.0 assessment, you can turn your eyes, your mind and your heart AWAY from your weaknesses. Instead, you get to focus on your greatest potential for strengths!

So let's get started.

Over the next week, you get to observe your life and discover concrete ways you are using your talents. You get to catch yourself in action.

DON'T SKIP THIS PART!

I understand your desire to move forward. However, you must not brush over this exercise.

When your talents are operating as strengths, you're being the very best version of yourself. YOU are, after all, the very best at being YOU.

It's your "zone" or your "sweet spot." It's the space where you are MASTER of your domain; the space in which you live, work or play. It's the place you were meant to shine with excellence and high productivity.

And if you can observe and figure out HOW YOU DO IT, you can do it again and again and again.

A friend of mine, Nichole, went to the lake one summer with some friends and rented a pontoon boat. They were parked next to another boat that seemed to have a lot of fun people on board.

One of the friends in her party said, "Nichole! Go over there and do that thing you do!" By that, she meant for Nichole to go over, break the ice and engage the people in the boat next door.

And that's exactly what Nichole did -- that "thing she did."

Well, you have "that thing" you do -- or those things

you do -- with similar mastery and excellence. So what are they?

In this exercise, write a few instances when you recognize or have recognized yourself "in action" and living in a talent as a strength.

Write each of your Top 5 talents below. Set your alarm on your phone to ring every three hours (while you're awake, of course). When it rings, pause and think about what you've done and what has happened over the past few hours and write down what worked and where you felt your best.

Look at this list every day for the next week. Add incidents, situations or occurrences where you know you were in your "zone."

Talent: _____

Observations:

_____

_____

_____

Talent: _____

Observations:

_____

_____

_____

Talent: _____

Observations:

_____

_____

_____

Talent: _____

Observations:

_____

_____

_____

Talent: _____

Observations:

_____

_____

_____

Chapter 4:

Discern Your Strengths

If you completed Chapter 3, you will have "caught" yourself living in your strengths. It's in those actions and activities where you shine with excellence and have great energy. You are UNSTOPPABLE!

It takes time to do that because, as I said earlier, you don't even notice how good you are at some things. You've been so busy looking at your weaknesses and trying to fix yourself that you've overlooked how awesome you are! By catching yourself "in the act" of a strength, you will get to discern how -- exactly -- you did that.

Did you walk into a meeting, an event or a party and touch as many people as possible -- especially new people?

Or did you find yourself in the corner catching up with people you know? Did you avoid the event altogether?

These may be clues.

Did you find yourself pouring over new reports or filling in the gaps in the structure of a new process or operation? Were you involved in any long-term planning projects or goal-setting sessions?

These could be clues, too.

Did you find yourself lost in your learning? Did you discover a new interest that had you gathering information for a time? Were you pulled into another history book or did you watch another documentary or two?

More clues.

Did you find yourself nurturing or teaching or comforting people? Solving problems or restoring order?

These are all clues as to where your strengths lie, and what gives you the most potential to achieving excellence and satisfaction in your day-to-day life. Paying attention to them will make you more aware of how powerful you are!

In this exercise, it's time to identify exactly what you do with ease and what drains you. By learning what sucks the life out of you, you'll discern exactly what you need to start outsourcing.

List the routine duties that you handle every day at home, at work or at play. To the right, indicate the Top 5 talent you think you're using.

Duty/Activity:	Talent Used

You may be using more than one talent to do specific duties -- in fact, it's likely that you're combining talents. While we often talk about our Top 5 in isolation, but most of us combine our talents in order to achieve results.

Do you find yourself leaning on one of your Top 5 more often than the others? The reason why may be another clue!

Chapter 5:

Develop Your Strengths

Exciting news: every talent you have is a potential strength!

Not so exciting news: every talent you have is a potential weakness.

Too bad someone can't come along and anoint you with strengths and in an instant, change your whole world for the better! It doesn't quite happen that way, does it?

Transformation CAN happen in an instant. Total change takes a lifetime. I hate to break it to you, but, if you're like most of us you'll be working on this the rest of your life!

The good news is that the tools you now have provide a new language and context for you to use to create a life by design. You get to continue along your journey and transform your way of life by honing and sharpening your natural talents.

And even better news -- it's a much easier way to live than trying to fix yourself!

Before we get started, let's make sure you understand the difference between a talent and a strength.

A talent is what you do naturally -- a recurring pattern of thoughts, feelings or behavior that can be applied to any situation. They exist within you and you do them automatically, instinctively. Talent cannot be taught. Talent is innate, inborn. Your talents are like the raw materials that you have to work within your life.

A strength is actually matured talent. It's when you have developed your talent to the point where you can provide positive and consistent performance in a given area. Near perfect performance. A strength is a powerful merging of talent, skill, knowledge and practice. It's the point where you have maximized your talent and are at the top of your game!

So, let's take a look at your Top 5 talents again and see if there are areas where you could stand a little improvement. (And let me assure you, you can always develop your top talents no matter how strong you think you are in them.)

Here's a list of the thirty-four StrengthsFinder talents, what they look like when developed, and their downside -- when they show up as a weakness. Let's call this living in the penthouse (strength) or the outhouse (weakness). I call it living in the "outhouse" because frankly you STINK. (I do, too, when I get tripped up and fall. We all do.)

Talent	Penthouse (Strength)	Outhouse (Weakness)
Achiever	High work ethic; very productive.	Works too much, can't relax; judges others for not producing.
Activator	Seizes opportunities & acts quickly; fearless.	Busy going nowhere fast; high anxiety with no activity.
Adaptability	Flexible in times of transition and change.	Won't make commitments; wishy-washy decision making.
Analytical	Analyzes data & numbers; thinks things through.	Analysis paralysis; always needs more data and time.
Arranger	Organizes & plans with great efficiency; flexible w/change.	Constantly changing for sake of efficiency; hard to follow.
Belief	Inner core values; honest, high integrity, family values.	Intolerant of other beliefs; judgmental.
Command	Excellent leader who brings clarity; clears chaos.	Bossy and dictator-ish. Insensitive to feelings of others.
Communication	Excellent presenter; good communicator; writer.	Overtalks & monopolizes conversation; doesn't listen.
Competition	Measurement driven; goes for the win.	Always competing; sore loser; cheats to win.
Connectedness	Deeply spiritual; sees all in life connected.	Connects random things that don't make sense.
Consistency	Strong sense of justice; creates/follows policies/ rules.	Rigid about rules and regulations; intolerant of rule breaking.

Talent	Penthouse (Strength)	Outhouse (Weakness)
Context	Deep understanding of past & how things came to be.	Gets locked in the past; can't move forward without back story.
Deliberative	Excellent at managing risk; sees potential risk & danger.	Gets fearful over negative possibilities; avoids action.
Developer	Nurtures potential in others; uplifting, empowering.	Wastes time on low performers; accepts excuses from others.
Discipline	Organized, orderly; brings timelines & structure.	Rigid about order; cannot handle change.
Empathy	Senses & feels what others are feeling; intuitive.	Oversensitive; can't regulate emotion.
Focus	Goal driven; ability to eliminate distractions.	Over focused on goals & misses the journey.
Futuristic	"Sees" possibilities 5, 10, 20 years into the future.	Gets locked in their heads; dreamer with little action.
Harmony	Excellent negotiator; brings peace and harmony.	Fearful of disharmony; won't speak truth or rock the boat.
Ideation	Creative; excellent in idea generation, brainstorming.	Shuts down if ideas not accepted. Lots of ideas, little action.
Includer	Inclusive; non-judgmental; sensitive to those on outside.	Indiscriminate when including others; gets taken advantage of.
Individualization	Sees uniqueness in others & how to place them for success.	Over-customizes solutions; frustrated by rules.
Input	Gathers, sorts & archives data and things; collector.	Tendency towards clutter; won't throw things away.
Intellection	Deep, philosophical thinker; introspective.	Over thinks; little action; loner, isolated, anti-social.

Talent	Penthouse (Strength)	Outhouse (Weakness)
Learner	Curious; loves process of learning; gathers knowledge.	Knowledgeable but little action; can't disseminate information.
Maximizer	Aims high; standard of perfection; outputs high quality.	Critical, perfectionistic, judgmental; alienates people.
Positivity	Happy, joyful, dramatic; uplifts others.	Delusional about reality; puts positive spin too quickly.
Relator	Deep relationships with close, inner circle.	Exclusionary; won't let others in.
Responsibility	Takes psychological ownership & ensures things get done.	Micromanages; righteous about how things are done.
Restorative	Sees broken patterns & systems and offers solutions.	Negative, critical; always looking at broken things; self-critical.
Self-Assurance	Independent leader guided by inner compass; confident.	Over-confident; arrogant.
Significance	Seeks excellence, recognition; legacy minded.	Grandstands; takes credit for other's work; name dropper.
Strategic	Intuitively sees the right path in problem solving.	Manipulative; won't share plan details.
WOO	High energy networker; connector.	Collects people indiscriminately; networks with no purpose.

In this exercise, you'll have a chance to recognize the greatest areas of growth to turn your talents into strengths. List your Top 5 talents and take an honest look at the outhouse view of each one. Write down areas where you see yourself living in strength and weakness.

Talent	Penthouse	Outhouse
Example: Communication	I'm good at presenting and storytelling.	I need to be a better listener & not talk all the time.

Chapter 6:
Strengths at Home

Whenever your strengths are revealed you can find yourself living in them across the whole of your life. You'll live in your talents at home -- perhaps in the handling of your children or in the ways the daily chores and household maintenance are handled. Maybe you keep the family calendar while your spouse handles the finances.

Regardless of where you use your talents at home, you're using them. Begin identifying them and you'll discover HOW you utilize them. Once you do that, you can -- deliberately and with intention -- do them again. This becomes your sweet spot -- those places and spaces that give you immense satisfaction and joy!

In this exercise, you will identify the ways you use

your Top 5 talents at home.

Top 5 talents:

_____

_____

_____

_____

_____

I find myself using the following talents doing routine things around my house or apartment:

_____

_____

_____

_____

When it comes to my home relationships, I discovered myself using the following talents in the following situations:

_____

_____

_____

_____

When it comes to the household budget and other financial considerations, my talents come into play in these ways:

_____

_____

_____

_____

I noticed that the talents I use the most at home are:

_____

_____

_____

_____

These are the areas at home in which I am not working with peak efficiency and excellence (think drudgery):

_____

_____

_____

_____

Chapter 7:
Strengths at Work

As mentioned earlier, your talents follow you throughout all of your life and your work is no exception.

Chances are if you're like most of us, you have found yourself in a job or work situation that finally pays the bills (or at least most of them), but perhaps it doesn't bring you complete fulfillment and satisfaction. We've all been there going from job to job through trial and error before finally "settling."

Do you really want to settle?

Perhaps you're really, really good at some of your job functions. And perhaps you're really, really not so good at some of them. Observation, once again, becomes your first key to change.

In this exercise, you get to take a look at your work situation and how your strengths are in operation. Take a look over the next several days at your job functions and how they are handled.

Top 5 Talents:

_____

_____

_____

_____

_____

I find myself using the following talents doing routine things on the job:

_____

_____

_____

When it comes to my work relationships, I discovered myself using the following talents in the following situations:

_____

_____

_____

When it comes to collaborating with other departments or companies during work, my talents come into play in these ways:

_____

_____

_____

I noticed that the talents I use the most at work are:

_____

_____

_____

Chapter 8:
Strengths at Play

Just as you use your gifts and talents at home and at work, you also use them at play. For the scope of this step and its exercises, let us consider "play" to be anything that is outside the bounds of your job or home life.

For example, you may be involved in a sports, music, or art activity after hours. Maybe you volunteer for a civic organization or at your church or faith community.

You could be working with children, or maybe you're an advocate for those less fortunate. Perhaps you arrange missions or possibly you are in fundraising for your favorite charity.

Regardless, you are using your gifts and talents across all aspects of your life -- including your play time. In this exercise, take a look at where you find your talents showing up in your extracurricular activities and play time.

Top 5 talents:

_____

_____

_____

_____

_____

These are the organizations that I am a part of (civic, business, philanthropy, networking, faith-based or missional):

_____

_____

_____

_____

_____

After looking, I see myself taking on the following roles within the group(s):

_____

_____

_____

_____

_____

When it comes to my relationships within these groups, I discovered myself using the following talents in the following situations:

_____

_____

_____

When it comes to collaborating with other committee members, my talents come into play in these ways:

_____

_____

_____

I noticed that the talents I use the most in these group(s) are:

_____

_____

_____

Chapter 9:
Embrace Your Strengths

Now it's time for you to deliberately put your talents to use.

By now, you should see a pattern emerging that shows who you are, and more importantly, how you do things best. You've discovered your best potential for strengths by taking the Gallup StrengthsFinder Assessment. You also know your Top 5 talents and you've learned what they mean.

You've followed the exercises and seen your talents in action. You've observed yourself during your duties and responsibilities at home, at work, and at play. A pattern has emerged with clues as to what you do best, what your sweet spot is, and where your best opportunities for excellence lie.

So, now that you know all this great stuff about yourself, you get an opportunity to put it in action! You get the chance to look at who you are and how you do things best and then do it -- this time on purpose!

First, take a look back in chapter 2 - Words that Resonate. Your Top 5 talents mean something, certain words and phrases jumped out at you and resonated with you. These are the power words of your life!

You also looked at your talents and gifts showing up in your day-to-day activities and responsibilities, at home, at work, and at play. These are all clues as to what you do best and, at the same time, what you do NOT do best.

With this in mind, let's ponder the future for a few minutes. In this exercise, let's take a look at your favorite things to do in life as well as the things you need to find alternative ways and means to get done. During the previous steps, you identified the things in your day-to-day activities where you saw your talents and strengths in action.

In the spaces provided, write which specific things you enjoy doing, that bring you fulfillment, satisfaction and joy:

_____

_____

_____

_____

_____

Why do these things make you happy? What is it, exactly, that brings that joy? Are you creating things? Are you helping people? Do you immerse yourself in learning? Jot down here what you think it is that brings about this feeling in you:

_____

_____

_____

_____

Where else in your life, in your home, in your church, in your community do you see a need for these things you do with excellence?

_____

_____

_____

_____

With which of your talents have you developed a greater appreciation?

_____

_____

_____

_____

_____

Why do you think you have a greater appreciation?

_____

_____

_____

_____

Chapter 10:
Strengthen Your Talents

As we discussed earlier, there's a difference between a talent and a strength. Sometimes, all you need to do to strengthen a talent is to get additional training, add more education, or just practice. Obviously, by adding this experience, you will be able to grow in knowledge and get better at all those great things you do!

It's important that you take responsibility for your own continued development. We have a few suggestions for you:

First, recognize that THIS IS THE WORK OF YOUR LIFE!

You're not going to be able to read a book or fill in the blanks on a workbook and suddenly have your life changed.

Although transformation can happen in an instant, change takes a lifetime.

Awareness can come about immediately. However, unless you take the time and energy to be intentional about understanding yourself and how you do things, you'll be slow to apply your new knowledge.

That said, there are some things you can do to continue your strengths-based journey.

Personal and Professional Development:

You are wired to learn and develop more easily when you focus on your natural talents. What kind of training do you need? What conferences and seminars should you attend?

Let's look at next steps by looking at your Top 5. For each talent, write down a possible skill you need to develop or training you need in order to grow forward.

Talent	Training/Skill Development
Example: Communication	Join ToastMasters; take writing course

And here are some other ways that you can continue to grow and develop your talents into strengths:

Plug in. Read other Strength-based materials published by the Gallup Strengths Center. There have been many books written about the work of Donald Clifton, the creator of the assessment, as well other authors associated with Gallup.

The Yellow Sub Group Blog: We also have a extensive information on our blog. You can find it here: www.YellowSubGroup.com/blog

The Podcast: There are many recordings of the Activate Your Strengths Show. These are interviews that I've done with various people helping us see how their talents show up in their lives. You can find it here: https://www.yellowsubgroup.com/category/podcast/

Take action. At the Gallup Strengths Center, you will find several reports to download about your particular talents and potential strengths. Especially look at the Action Planning Guide and choose one new thing to implement now. Once you've mastered one, move on to another.

Join us. I highly recommend attending the workshops frequently offered in Oklahoma City, Oklahoma. You can learn more about them here: www.YellowSubGroup.com.

Build Community. Grow your own community by inviting others to learn their Top 5 talents and getting them involved. When you have company along with you, your journey becomes a shared experience that helps others grow, too. Creating a "common language" with StrengthsFinder will benefit everyone around you!

The End -- but Just the Beginning!

In closing, thanks for allowing me to join you -- however -- briefly -- on your journey. I know you are looking for something that will change the direction of your life, and I believe that a strengths-based approach will do just that.

I've seen the evidence of powerful change and transformation in the lives of many -- including my own. And my hope for you is that you realize that you're on a journey and that you will -- one step at a time -- move forward into the very best version of YOU.

Our world needs your talents and gifts. More importantly, we need your strengths!

61